Suncatcher

SUNCATCHER

Susannah White

Edited by Derek Healy

Graffiti Books

Suncatcher
Susannah White

Published by Graffiti Books 2021
Malvern, Worcestershire, United Kingdom
Email: graffitibooksuk@gmail.com
Website: www.graffitibooks.uk

Graffiti Books is the book publishing arm of *Graffiti Magazine*

Printed and bound by Aspect Design
89 Newtown Road, Malvern, Worcs. WR14 1PD
United Kingdom
Tel: 01684 561567
E-mail: allan@aspect-design.net
Website: www.aspect-design.net

ISBN 978-1-9163339-2-5

In memory of my writing friend, Richard Hensley:

Visions flash on his inner eyes
Of times and places not his own.
Of peoples yet to live, to die
Of many futures yet to come.

Words of past and words of wonder
Meanings just beyond his knowing.
Words of future, words to ponder
Flood his mind and raise his voice.
                              (Richard Hensley)

Contents

About the Poet

Susannah White was born in 1964 and grew up by the coast in Dawlish, Devon. Her love of the sea often permeates her poetry. After studying English and Drama at Swansea University, she had some success as a fiction writer, being shortlisted for the Ian St James Awards in 1991. Her focus changed from prose to poetry when she joined the Dewsbury Writers in Yorkshire, publishing her first volume of poetry *Shall I?* with Spout Publications in 1996.

Susannah trained as an English teacher at Southampton University then studied for an M.A. in Writing for Children at King Alfred's College, Winchester. Since 2002, she has lived in Cirencester, Gloucestershire, where she is a keen member of two local writing groups: Catchword and the Cirencester Thursday evening writing group. Now retired, she enjoys writing by lakes at the Cotswold Water Park whilst her husband, Steve, fishes. Susannah was longlisted for the international Erbacce Poetry Prize in 2020 and won the national Swanwick Writing School poetry competition in 2015.

MEMORIES

Suncatcher

Today I caught the sun
and smeared it across my page in coloured chalk.
There was a poet on the bench to the left of me
but for once it seemed permissible not to talk.

The art teacher showed me how to shape the sea
by rubbing out the shading I had done.
The more I drew, the more I knew that poetry
lay in the place where I had caught the sun.

This poem was first published in *Chasing the Horizon*
(Catchword Writing Group, 2017).

Dada

(After my son, Tom's, first word)

Da is the answer to the universe,
Da is the question too.
Da is a teddy bear.
A rubber duck.
Da is the bottle of milk
which we give to you
when we put you to sleep
with your da special blanket.
Da is bananas and Weetabix,
Da is the phone you climb to reach:
Da grandma
Da grandpa
Da sister
Da brother
Da mother.
But you know your father's name.
You call him
Dada.

This poem was first published in *To Dads with Love,*
(GMGA Publishing, 2021).

Eggs

Our shoulders touch
as we stand outside the chicken hutch.
Then you step in,
emerging with four perfect eggs
cradled in your hand.

You pass me one,
oval as the rugby balls
our boys are sending flying
across the lawn.

We must fly too,
running to catch a train of thought
that comes to us out of the blue,
miraculous as the eggs
and carried as carefully.

Child in the Garden

(For Emma)

In the garden, where you stand,
I watch the soft rose petals land.
They glide and sail across the air,
and one or two fall in your hair.

I think of how I've watched you play,
in some sweet magic world all day,
your easy grace, your eyes so clear;
how blessed I feel to have you near.

Now it is late and time to go.
I love you more than you can know,
but words can't hold my love, not all
I feel for you, as petals fall.
The petals shine like angel's wings,
if we could just believe such things.

This poem was first published in *Poetic Treasures*
(United Press, 2015).

At College

Friday afternoon in the autumn sun.
Nearly everyone is outside, on the grass.

Here, an impressionist scene of dappled light,
artists and scientists as one.
A photographer might catch them
with pink hair and rainbow boots.

This is an optimistic place
for those who dream of being famous soon,
and on this dazzling, sunny afternoon of golden trees
it seems that everything is possible
for some of these.

This poem has previously been published in *South
and South West England* (Forward Press, 2009) and in
Chasing the Horizon (Catchword Writing Group, 2017).

Bus World

Welcome to the bus world.
The late night intimacy
of sleepy strangers,
young girls in mini skirts
and drunks who sing.

A man on his mobile phone,
an old lady clearing her throat,
as a coke can
rolls down the aisle.

Now a student in a brown hat,
a lady muttering in Japanese,
a bearded man
and the can

rolling back again.

This poem was first published in
Contrasting Visions (United Press, 2015).

University Studies

At night he opens the window,
turns on the light
and waits till the moths fly in.

Then he catches them under a glass,
looks them up in books,
photographs their eyes
and the patterns of their wings.

By morning he feels exhausted.
He lifts the glass and lets the last moth fly.
Then, wearily, he makes his way to lectures
where he cannot catch the words
and doesn't try.

This poem was first published in
The Cannon's Mouth, issue 59 (2016).

The Beach Hut

(For Catherine, who bought a beach hut
on eBay for £20 to use as a writing retreat)

This wooden hut
once stood beside the sea,
our special place
to share a cup of tea
after the swims
we noted on its walls
. . . as marks of history.

And then, one day,
we plucked it from its perch,
entrusted it to you,
who knew its worth
(far more than twenty pounds)
for this rebirth,
worked at its heart
to save a sense of sanctuary.

Flash Drive

(After scanning old photographs)

Memory sticks
on USB,
scanned photos
pass at a click.
Dead strangers:
friends of your mother's brother,
silver jubilee, fairground and beach.
Kids on space hoppers.
Pack-a- mac picnic,
carnival and pier.
Your sister on the steps
as a brownie
as a bride.
Grandma in her bubble car,
waiting for a drive.

This poem was first published in *Chasing the Horizon*
(Catchword Writing Group, 2017).

The People from My Past

The people from my past
float out of an old address book
on post-it notes.
For years now I've sent them cards without reply.
I write my address for return
but they don't come back.

Some of them may have moved house –
they could even be dead –
but today they fly
across my living room
and I try to catch them.

This poem was first published in
The Cannon's Mouth, issue 78 (2020).

Stranger in the Graveyard

(After a visit to Painswick churchyard
in Gloucestershire)

Amongst our stones you wander in a haze;
and on our bones you wonder as you gaze
upon our tombs, our strong, impressive graves,
our chambers and our tables – not alone.
And there are more – where moss and lichen grow;
and there are more – cherub encrusted rows;
and some have flowers and some are decked in bows.
But you are none, no, you are none of those.
You are like stone.

This poem was first published in
The Cannon's Mouth, issue 59 (2016).

Searching for Meteors
(In memory of Richard Hensley)

That night after the party
we searched for meteors
in a half drunk sky.

In the dregs of your wine
I noticed a fly
floating . . .
or maybe that was me
or a plane
or a planet
or a figure drifting across the grass.

Somebody told us
that he had seen a meteor
but they move incredibly fast...

. . . as the fly floated
the night faded for me
so I left you peering upwards
stopping only
to tip the wine drenched fly
out
into the shrubbery.

This poem has previously been published in *Graffiti*,
issue 19 (2016) and *Chasing the Horizon*
(Catchword Writing Group, 2017).

POETRY

Bright Star
(for Keats)

Bright star, you are still constant in the sky –
against the backdrop of another night
and on your stage, performing in this play
are manmade echoes of your greater light.
The rushing headlamps and the paths of planes
send horns and sonic booms to hurt your ears,
or strange fluorescence, rising out of football games
played after dark with artificial cheers.
No – yet still steadfast, still unchangeable
listening to our broadcasts and our beats
to hear forever their harsh rise and fall
in teenage cars careering down our streets.
Still, still, you watch and wait. Shine and inspire
the poets who search for silence in your fire.

This poem was first published in *The Cannon's Mouth*
issue 59 (2016). It was also part of an unnamed
collection longlisted for the Erbacce Poetry Prize, 2020.

Juno

(From Virgil's *The Aeneid*, Book 1)

Juno, daughter of Saturn,
had not forgotten Troy.
Its battles like bitter resentments
marked her mind.

The judgement of Paris,
her beauty had been denied;
and Jupiter, her husband,
preferred Ganymede at his side
as cupbearer and friend.

How she hated the stock of Dardanus,
how she wished they'd met their end
with Achilles and the Greeks.
Of course they were fated to wander,
but she knew what they'd come to seek
and she longed for their losses to be heavy.

Out of sight of Sicily
heading for the open sea
the Trojans sailed happily
their spirits rising high.

But Juno, in her darkest mood,
continued to conspire and brood.
The scars of battle burned like hate,
she'd bring them down,
she'd challenge fate.

For in the past,
when Ajax sinned,
hadn't the Gods
with fire and wind
attacked his fleet
thrown flames to sea

until they saw his body
impaled upon a jagged rock?

Bring whirlwinds, thunderbolts
but stop.

I fear that people cease to pray to me.
Is that an empty altar that I see?
I am the Queen of Gods.
I am the Queen.

This poem was part of an unnamed collection
longlisted for the Erbacce Poetry Prize, 2020.

Sister without Mercy

(A modern version of Keats's 'La Belle Dame Sans Merci')

She sings
on sound waves to me.
'I know who you are,
I know who you want to be . . .'

Her blank-faced backing men
repeat, repeat,
a mesmerising beat,
as bird tattoos fly around arms,
strumming an electric guitar.

Her bangles jangle with charms,
for the final riff,
one last refrain.

I'm drawn towards the stage,
through pouring rain,
because she's holding out

a smile,
on the palm of her hand.

I place it on my tongue,
watch a sun sinking
into ecstasy . . .

I'm waking up,
        breaking up,
as backstage boys
take flood lights down.

I'm staggering
through muddy fields,
making my way back to town
with other pale-faced men.

Sister without mercy.
It was not just me.

An earlier version of this poem was part of an
unnamed collection longlisted for
the Erbacce Poetry Prize, 2020.

Daffodils by the Lake

Did William Wordsworth sit beside this lake
and watch its waters shimmering with light?
This is a place of pure tranquillity
where mirrored mountains kiss the moon by night.

But it is morning now, and I'm alone,
except for one keen climber on the hills,
so I must leave my seat of mossy stone,
and go in search of dancing daffodils.

Then suddenly a host of them appear,
close to the lake beside the budding trees;
from half a life away I clearly hear
those golden voices calling on the breeze.
Though I am old, I still recall that poem.

I take a photo – flowers fill my phone.

This poem was first published in *Ways to Peace: Tintern Abbey, Wales* (On the Edge Publishing, 2019). It was also part of an unnamed collection longlisted for the Erbacce Poetry Prize, 2020.

On Finding Dylan in a Boarding School Library

A hardback book of poems by Dylan Thomas,
The pages yellow- brown and underlined
By studious pencils neath the library clock
Salvaged from some lost treasury of time.

Row after row of anxious, frazzled looks
And scratching pens, and writing tight and neat.
Row after row of ancient, dusty books.
The grave stole Dylan's breath but not his beat.

Here, where his 'seathumbed leaves' have lain in sleep,
Out of some 'kindled' darkness Dylan wakes
To ink stained fingers marked with due by dates
And clicking heels in place of fishing hooks.

Row after row of ancient, dusty books,
And eyes of walls and frames and wooden birds.
The grave stole Dylan's breath but not his beat.
A raging beat that burns in me like words.

This poem was published in *Graffiti,* issue 16 (2014) and *Crystal,* issue 122 (2021). It was also part of an unnamed collection longlisted for the Erbacce Poetry Prize, 2020.

Prospero's Song

I made this tempest, shaped it with my rage,
but, sweet Miranda, I did it for you.
Love and revenge will meet upon this stage.
Behold the brave and bold, the old and new.
How innocent you are of worldly things;
the island has been gentle in this way,
whilst I, who've mixed with emperors and kings
must draw the final curtain on our play.
Blow tempest then, drive them towards this shore,
lash them until they scream, with hail and rain.
Come dreadful thunder; let me hear you roar,
make them bow down to Prospero again.

My enemies approach, in disarray;
so wake, Miranda, let us watch the play.

This poem was first published in
Sonnets for Shakespeare (Forward Poetry, 2015).

CREATIVITY

Odette

After her fall
she left the ballet
and went to live
with a man who sent her flowers.

Her fame faded
to the pages of a scrapbook,
tangled tights at the back of a drawer,
a plastic wrapped tutu
hanging behind her door,
a cracked tiara.

Yet still she posed on his arm
in rose scented satin and lace,
silver hair swept back from her face
in a ballerina's bun.

Her sequinned shoes still shone,
but her thoughts flailed and fluttered
like the dying swan
on her mind's music.

Ice Dance

When we were young I loved him;
now we are brother and sister on ice,
his face pressed close to mine,
bodies turning . . .

. . . arms around my waist,
legs tangling together
for years
living out of a suitcase.

There is always space,
another city,
another rink.

I must let go of his hand
at the barrier.

An earlier version of this poem was published
in *Shall I?* (Spout Publications, 1996).

Where Do We Meet?

Where do we meet?
Love is a dangerous word
yet the connection between us
runs deep.

I hear the still, soft voice
and paint it as gentle, crimson roses
with dark leaves
for that's what it feels like
at our meeting place.

You and I have
no interests in common,
we are not the same age.
What can I say? I wait . . .
The voice whispers, 'Trust'.

Stranger
I'm frightened to step across
our unmarked barrier,
but I know I must . . . .

This poem was first published in
The Friend, issue unknown (1991).

Colourless

Today the sky is white
and I don't understand why
because it is nearly night
on a summer's day.
It is as white as the wine in my hand
as I sit outside
trying to understand
why we have whiteness.

Right now I want a Jackson Pollock fling
colours mixing
art in   juxtaposition
        pink and black and blue
                ink blots with butterfly wings
        a cacophony of light
spilling out across this blank flat canvas
        and taking flight.

This poem was longlisted for the Paragram Poetry
Award and published in their anthology
Slants of Light: Paragram (Four Point Press, 2013).

Block Printing

Take a lino block,
carve the night sky.
Think in reverse;
uncut areas carry colour.
Add scratches for interest.
Squeeze ink into a tray,
roll on and off . . .
Place paper on top,
press with a wooden spoon
then peel away,
to see
spaces
where stars should be.

This poem was highly commended in the
Creative Manchester Poetry Competition, 2021.

Millington Exhibition

(Museum in the Park July, 2015)

Blue bird,
blue bottle and bluebell.
A bowl of oranges,
a 'two plate etching' of dogs
and the River Dart, dark and gloomy.
A spade – lawnmower wall with the shadow of trees
and always a vase – in willow pattern perhaps
. . . maybe Chinese . . .

And how do the grapes drape themselves?
And how do the pears declare femininity?
And what is the relationship between vase and shell,
or
garlic and red chillies
or between
blue bird, blue bottle and bluebell.

This poem was first published in *Chasing the Horizon*
(Catchword Writing Group, 2017).

Plasticine

(For Pamela Harbutt)

I loved it when it was new
sandwiched in cellophane
brightly coloured, slightly sticky bars,
squished it into softness
growing warm under my palm.

I couldn't resist
mixing colours to make mottled marbles
and meals for dolls house teas.

Tiny green peas slipped through my fingers.
I found them days later
impaled in the carpet.

Mostly I rolled out snakes,
wound round
to make flat snail shell mats.

After a while everything turned brown.

If I could have another go
I might model The Muses
or the Venus de Milo.

This poem was first published in
The Cannon's Mouth, issue 78 (2020).

Song for a Daughter

Give me a yarrow leaf
and I will make you a pendant
of silver clay – its impression in relief.

Find me a feather
and I will sew you a Native American headdress
for your tepee at forest school.

Bring me willow
and I will weave you a basket
for gathering sticks and twigs.

Take me to a clearing
and we will sit together on chopped logs
whittling time away by the fire.

Mosaic Maker

She scavenges in skips,
forages through rubbish tips for fragments of
    patterned plates,
searches the beach for smooth green glass.

Later, in her studio, she washes off grime,
taking time to separate colours
before leaving them to rest.

Next day, she sketches waves and sand
on a round wooden board,
spreads silicone across its surface,
arranging mirror tiles, china and shattered shells
before applying grout.

When she wipes the excess away
a shimmering mother-of-pearl mermaid
bobs up from the willow patterned sea.

This poem was a runner up in the Horwich Creative
Mind competition published in their *Transformation:
An Anthology from Creative Mind* (PreeTa Press, 2021).

WATER

The Lake

(Covid lockdown 2020)

I long to sit beside a fishing lake,
and spend my time watching the ducks drift by.
No fears or doubts,
no piles of bills to pay,
no-one to take offence
at what I do
or say.

My lake will sparkle
in the morning sun.
My only focus will be catching fish.
Fears and resentments will be lost
then gone.
Time by a fishing lake is all I wish.

This poem was first published in
When This is All Over (Creative Ink Publishing, 2021).

Ripples

Ripples spread around the orange float.
These circles of our worlds are muddy green
and Monet might have painted in their light
across reflected trees
and leaves floating on
a silver soup
of hope.

This poem was first published in
Graffiti, issue 18 (2015).

Beside the Lake

(For Steve)

The wine touches my lips
but I must wait for the moment when it hits
as ripple rings, and bubbles from fish
break the surface
of the lake.

I take another sip,
and then
one brave duck sneaks up
to steal a piece of corn
from underneath your fishing tray.

When the corn is gone
he waddles away
like me in your huge green boots
too lazy to squeeze into my own tight shoes
because they have to be removed
each time I go inside
to fetch more wine.

This poem was first published in *Chasing the Horizon,*
(Catchword Writing Group, 2017).

The Pool

There is only ceiling
white with blistering paint.

Suspended on the surface
of the water
she lies inside a blue mosaic frame.

There is only ceiling
buoyant in her mind,
a rippling path of warm fluorescent light.

Floating between her legs
as she spreads them,
the skin of the pool resisting
only ceiling.

This poem was first published in *Shall I?*
(Spout Publications, 1996).

Life in a Shoe Box

I will place the last of my life in a shoe box.
A photo, a notebook, a pressed leaf.
Less is more,
that is a core belief.

One day I'll live in a small place
beside the sea,
shedding a possession every week,
and when a shoe box is all that remains of me
I'll go swimming.

This poem was first published in
The Cannon's Mouth, issue 59 (2016).

The Gentle Waves

The tide is climbing up the beach;
    the crowds have gone away.
I stand alone on the sea wall
    and smile across the bay.
The sun is soothing on my face
    as I gaze out to sea.
Though it has been a busy day,
    I've found tranquillity.
The gentle waves caress my mind;
    wash over shell and stone,
then they retreat back down the beach,
    but I am not alone,
for soon they will return again –
    and then pull back once more.
I hear them picking pebbles up
    to scatter on the shore,
and all these little pebbles, touched by water,
    start to shine,
an act of transformation which reflects
    and mirrors mine.
For I was weary from my work,
    when I came to this wall,
but now my mind flies like the gulls
    and rises like their call.
A little seaside cafe waits;
    I smell fresh ground coffee
but as I leave, I still believe
    the waves will stay with me.

This poem was first published in
Ripples in Verse (United Press, 2016).

The Lap of Waves

The pebbles are washed by the sea.
It picks them up and throws them down,
carries them away
and moves them round.

They clatter and rattle free
till the tide turns,
leaving them in the soft lap of waves.

I am a wave,
crashing against the shore.
Ask for what you want
and I will bring you more . . .

A girl of three
runs along the water's edge.
Her eyes are meditations
calm and blue.

She fills her bucket with sand,
pats it down with a small brown hand.
Then starts collecting pebbles;
some of them won't do . . .
she likes it when they shine.

I am a wave,
crashing against the shore.
Ask for what you want
and I will bring you more . . .

Half-shrouded in mist
an old woman waits for the child
near the edge of the cliff.

Soon they'll be gone,
scattering pebbles,
even the ones that shone.

The Imaginary Friend

I'm back on the beach
and there's the child again,
with her golden curls
and rosebud dress.

'Remember me?' she says.
'I bet you thought I was dead!'

I can't reply.

'Haven't you missed me?'
'Don't you want to hug and kiss me?'

I nod and hold out my hand
but she scampers away.

'How could you think I was dead
when we share the same name?'

I run after her, gasping for breath,
until she clambers onto a
'king of the castle' rock.

'I've watched you from trees,
danced down your street on the breeze,
I've swung from your green garden gate.'

I lift her into my arms
but she giggles and wriggles away.

'Let's play!'

'Stop, wait . . . .'

That's her game.

'How could you think I was dead?
When we share the same name!'

.

DREAMS

I Open the Gate

I open the gate,
flakes of gold paint on my fingers,
dark trees,
trunks without branches,
a mocking bird
mocking,
hear the song, hear the song.
She is eating the apple.

Such eyes,
blue energy,
her naked body brown with earth,
hair muddy.
She brings me paints from berries and flowers.
Slowly I take off my stockings
then my dress.

A yellow finger smears across my cheeks,
diamonds on my belly,
snakes and birds fly from shoulders,
stars on my back.

She wants me to share the apple but I can't.

This poem was first published in *Shall I?*
(Spout Publications, 1996).

Reflections in a Glass Apple

He gives her a glass apple.
She holds it in her hand
watches the way he watches
her watching the light.
Bright eyes
eyes dazzling
eyes which he thinks are green
green in the glass of the apple
eyes of glass
glass eyes growing
stretching and growing
stretching around the curved skin
of a glass apple
as she rolls it gently in the palm
of a smooth white hand
and smiles.

This poem was first published in
The New Forest Poetry Society: Anthology 1996,
issue unknown (1996).

Warning against the Adulteress

(After Proverbs 7)

I watch the rain
falling in season.
There is peace for a moment
in our land.
Larders are full
and bellies are heavy
but we stand on the boundary
longing for a wilderness of shifting sand.

She lives down the street;
she works in the office;
she dances through my dreams
with her brazen face.
I know that her house is by the cemetery
but tonight
I have drawn the blind.

This poem was first published in *Shall I?*
(Spout Publications, 1996).

Breaking the Sabbath

We ran across the beach
to the arcade and stood there
waiting to see our pennies drop.

My sister said,
'We shouldn't be here on a Sunday'
but I wouldn't stop.

That day we
wanted to hear the sea.

High tide touched my toes
bare feet and tangled hair.
'Where have you been?'
God asked.
'Dangling from the pier.'

This poem was first published in *Spokes*, 23 May 1993.

Slick

Something moves on the shore.
It is a dark shape.
I am not sure
of its meaning.

The shadow
which brings change.
The menace
of a strange
disconnected claw.
Dead crab
served on a slab
of polystyrene.

The wing
of a blackened bird.
The phoenix
which will not rise
before it has entered
thick, black dirt.

And man
on his line of sand
can't turn back tides
but slides
easily into
the shadow.

This poem was a runner up in the Horwich Creative Mind
competition and was published in *Nature and Nurture and Walking
in Nature – An Anthology from Creative Mind* (PreeTa Press, 2020).

Surfing the Severn Bore

You told me we could surf the Severn bore,
ride on a wave for more than half an hour,
and I agreed, although I wasn't sure
if we were skilled enough to face its power.

We checked a calendar for the best date,
then hired a boat to follow the wave's course.
The captain took us out to lie in wait
on surfboards . . . till it met us with full force.

We managed to stand up, held out our arms,
then felt its rushing waters fast and free,
gliding past corn, then cattle, sheep and farms
as we rode on its crest in harmony
with its great strength – a strength we'd never known,
which in that instant had become our own.

This poem was first published in *Ways to Peace:
Tintern Abbey, Wales* (On the Edge Publishing, 2019).

Catchword

(A friend told me that birds keep flying at her
windows leaving oily imprints on the glass – in the
dream world her birds became my words.)

A pigeon smashes against my window.
A word remains trapped behind glass.
Imprint of feathers in oil,
of pen in ink.

The garden is a battleground of birds.
Words fly then sink.
There are no mirrors,
for a sparrow doesn't know itself
and must attack
and a word is no reflection
of the thoughts
which arise
and then fly back.

This poem was first published in
The Cannons Mouth, issue 61 (2016).

To the Flame

Time and again
the moth
flies at the light.

The man turns to the bottle.
It feels good.
It feels right.

Such illumination,
such ascendency,
such pain.

But even as it burns,
he's driven back to it again.

The man is waxing lyrical tonight,
but with flaming wings
the moth
falls.

TRANSFORMATION

I Want to Be a Butterfly

It can be done.
I who have crawled dejected
through the drooping leaves,
despised and ready to be trodden on,
I can change.

I am ugly and despised.
hiding amongst the weeds,
crawling beside the wall,
wondering what lies in the world
beyond my cabbage patch.

All is humiliation,
life seems mostly black.
What am I to do?

I wrap myself up
in a cocoon of misery and cry . . .

Emerging,
through my fears,
I find I've grown bright wings.
Now I can fly.

This poem was a runner up in the Horwich Creative
Mind competition published in their *Transformation:
An Anthology from Creative Mind* (PreeTa Press, 2021).

First Thoughts

I want to brave the daylight some time.
I badly need to find
an opening
but most of all
to taste the air.
Somebody's taking off her clothes
down there.
Through the commotion I can hear
my Mum crying.

I'm pushing against the
slimy purple walls.
Somebody calls out in agony,
everything spins.

Then the white coats
are smeared with Mother's blood
and life begins.

This poem was first published in *Spokes,* 23 May 1993.

Blind Faith

I place a faceless angel on my tree.
She's getting old yet she remains serene.
She doesn't seem to show her age, like me;
unchanged, untouched by tragedies unseen.
Her wings reflect the sparking fairy lights;
each Christmas she seems brighter than before,
as if dark days and even darker nights
locked in a box can't hurt her any more.

Her hands are clasped perpetually in prayer.
Although there are no features on her face,
somehow I'm always conscious she is there,
raised high above me in her rightful place.
I take her down to put her out of mind,
yet she will rise again. Her faith is blind.

This poem was a runner up in the *Graffiti* sonnet
competition published in *Graffiti,* issue 22 (2018).

Peeling an Onion

I am peeling an onion
removing the outer skin.

I am peeling an onion
waiting for tears to sting,

but there are no tears
in this onion.

It is a bud
It is a flower opening.

I am peeling
I am revealing the flesh.

I am slicing it,
easing it apart.
I am splitting it at the centre
I am dividing it at the heart
I am cutting it
into neat, white pieces

This poem was the winner of the Swanwick National
Poetry Competition published in *Writing Magazine,* 2015.

Composting

This is a kind of ceremony –
the way we carry our little tray
to the compost bin
carefully lifting the lid
and pouring the contents in,
mixing,
wishing . . .

This is a sort of prayer.
Take these fragments to be broken
        and buried.
Take these shattered egg shells,
these stones from
        forgotten cherries.
Take them and make them into
        something more.
Take the heads of dead roses,
and my last summer strawberry.
Take them all.
Take them and make them greater
to enrich the earth
where I'll work with them,
turning them gently
to bring rebirth.

This poem was first published in *Ways to Peace:
Tintern Abbey, Wales* (On the Edge Publishing, 2019).

The Oak

I am standing in your cities,
I am part of country halls.
You can eat upon my tables.
You can climb over my walls.

My roots are wrapped in history,
my arms embrace the sun.
I am shaped, and smoothed and softened
by the things that you have done.

I am in your painted landscapes.
I am carved as modern art.
I'm the silent, wooden eagle
in the church within your heart.

I am driftwood on your beaches.
I am in your barns and beams.
I am fuel to light the fires
of this nation and its dreams.

This poem was first published in *The People's Friend
Fireside Book* (D. C. Thomson & Co, 2017).

Gatsby – The Magician

When you caught that clock
time stopped
allowing me to return
to your party tricks,
to the stories you kept spinning
like conjuring rings,
to a last garland,
a chain of white flowers – already dead
but still floating
in circles on the surface
of your green pool then
vanishing.

This poem was first published in
The Great Gatsby Anthology (Silver Birch Press, 2015).

Acknowledgements

I would like to express my gratitude to Derek Healy (my editor) and the other talented members of Catchword writing group (Liz Carew, Meg Davis-Berry, Gill Garrett, Rona Laycock, Pamela Keevil, Pamela Harbutt, Jan Turk Petrie, and Wilkie Martin) for their valuable feedback and encouragement. The members of my new Cirencester Thursday evening writing group have been highly supportive.

I have also benefited from sharing my goals and ideas with writers from Swanwick Summer School (especially Bea Charles, Joan Dowling and Linda Payne), Fishguard Writing Holiday and Lois Maddox's Relax and Write courses.

I am grateful for the inspiration provided by the following books on the craft of writing: Natalie Goldberg's *Wild Mind* (Rider, 1991) and *Writing Down the Bones* (Shambhala Publications, 2005), Julia Cameron's *The Artist's Way* (Pan Books, 1994), Peter Elbow's *Writing with Power* (OUP, 1998) and Jenny Alexander's *Writing in the House of Dreams* (Five Lanes Press, 2017) which encouraged me to include dream poems in this collection.

Many of the poems in this volume have appeared elsewhere and I am grateful to the magazines and anthologies who have published them.

Last, but not least, I would like to thank my family: Steve, Tom and Joe who are not as fond of poetry as I am, but often inspire it.